D0597951

Adoption

NOV 0 1 2002

LET'S TALK ABOUT IT

Adoption

FRED ROGERS

PHOTOGRAPHS BY JIM JUDKIS

The Putnam & Grosset Group

THIS BOOK IS THE PROPERTY OF
THE NATIONAL CITY PUBLIC LIBRARY
CHILDREN'S ROOM

Special thanks to Hedda Bluestone Sharapan for research and development; Barry N. Head, Susan Freivalds, and all of the friends and professionals who gave us guidance, and who shared some of their most personal thoughts and experiences with us.

We would also like to extend our special thanks to those adoptive families who graciously welcomed us into their homes and allowed us to photograph them for this book.

Printed on recycled paper

Text and photographs copyright © 1994 by Family Communications Inc.
All rights reserved. This book, or parts thereof, may not be reproduced in any form without permission in writing from the publisher.
A PaperStar Book, published in 1998 by The Putnam & Grosset Group,
200 Madison Avenue, New York, NY 10016.
PaperStar is a registered trademark of The Putnam Berkley Group, Inc.
The PaperStar logo is a trademark of The Putnam Berkley Group, Inc.
Originally published in 1994 by G. P. Putnam's Sons.
Published simultaneously in Canada. Printed in the United States of America.
Project Director: Margy Whitmer. Designed by Jackie Schuman
Text set in Korinna

Library of Congress Cataloging-in-Publication Data
Rogers, Fred
Adoption/by Fred Rogers;   photographs by Jim Judkis.
p.   cm.—(First Experiences)
Summary: Discusses what it means to be part of a family and examines some feelings that adopted children may have.
1. Adoption—Juvenile literature.   [1. Adoption. 2. Family.]
I. Judkis, Jim, ill.   II. Title.   III. Series: Rogers, Fred. Let's Talk About It.
HV875.R59   1993   362.7'34—dc20   92-15607   CIP   AC
ISBN 0-698-11625-9
1   3   5   7   9   10   8   6   4   2

What is a "family"?

My sister was adopted into our family when I was eleven years old. My mother and father became her mother and father. All of a sudden I was no longer an "only child" in the family. Understanding all of that came very gradually for me—and for my sister.

Different children find different ways to handle their feelings about adoption: How they want to talk about it, or even *if* they want to talk about it, will be an individual decision.

You, of course, know your child best, so I hope you will adapt the ideas in this book for him or her. That's one of the reasons we call this series of books "Let's Talk About It." It's an invitation for you and your child to take what we offer and talk about it in your own ways…ways that feel right for you and your family.

"Let's Talk About It" is also a way of saying that when we share our uncertainties (even about difficult things) with people who care about us, we often find that our feelings can be much more manageable. Even when there aren't answers, it can help just to know that the people we love care about our questions and the feelings that go along with them.

That's what your family really is—a group of people who care about who you are deep inside. Bloodlines and love lines don't necessarily coincide. When it comes to growing into a healthy, whole, and fulfilled human being, it is love that counts the most.

Fred Rogers

When you were born, you were ready to live and be loved, just like every other child in the world.

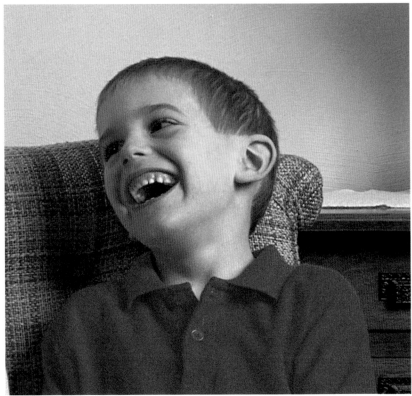

And you needed to be in a family, just like every other child in the world.

Being in a family means belonging...belonging because you are loved and cared for—

and because you give
love and give care, too.

You could belong in your family by being born into it, or you could belong in your family by being adopted into it.

You're an important part of your family. And the story of how you came into your family will always be important, too. In fact, it's a special kind of love story. Your family needed and wanted a child to love and care for, and you needed a family to love and care for you.

Everybody has lots of feelings about being in a family. There are times when you feel happy.

And there are times when you don't feel happy.

There can be angry times, like when your mom or dad says "no" to you and times when you feel like saying "no" to them.

But it can help to know there are angry times in *all* families and that people can still love each other, even if they get angry with each other once in a while. Being angry doesn't mean that love goes away.

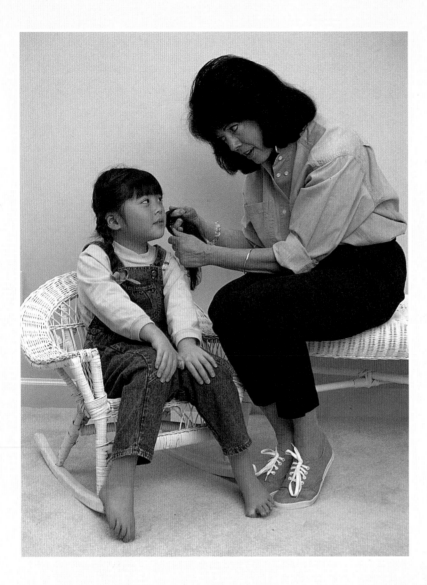

There may also be some times when you wonder about being adopted. Some children who are adopted wonder why they couldn't stay with their birthparents.

There can be many different reasons for that, and those reasons all have to do with grown-ups, not with anything a child did.

It can help to talk with your family about whatever you're wondering, even if your mom or dad sometimes says, "I don't know" or "Maybe you'll understand when you're older." Talking is a part of loving, and whatever you want to talk about means a lot to your family.

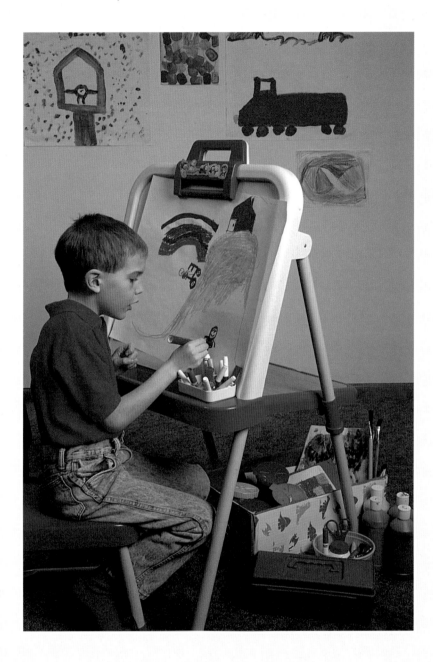

It can help to draw pictures, too.

Or pretend about being a mother or a father or a baby.

Playing is a good way to help you know more about families…and more about a lot of things.

There are so many times you can feel close to the people in your family...times when you go places together,

times when you help
around the house,

times when you have celebrations,

times when you share
quiet moments,

times when you laugh together,

and times when you comfort each other.

Your family is special because of all the ways you belong together.

And belonging can give everyone such a good feeling!